GOETHE INSTITUT

The Royal Court Theatre

in association with the
Goethe-Institut London

presents

WAITING ROOM GERMANY

by Klaus Pohl

translated by David Tushingham

Background to the International Programme at the Royal Court

When we examine the past of the English Stage Company, we can see that the international aspect of the work goes back to the beginning. It is significant that in 1956, when the Royal Court became the home of new theatre writing in this country, the first new international play to be produced in Sloane Square came from Germany. It was the British premiere of Bertolt Brecht's *The Good Woman of Setzuan* directed by George Devine, with a cast that included Peggy Ashcroft, John Osborne and Joan Plowright. This was followed through the late fifties and early sixties by productions of new plays by international writers such as Samuel Beckett, Max Frisch, Jean Genet, Eugene Ionesco, Arthur Miller and Wole Soyinka.

In the nineties new international writing continues to flourish at the Royal Court. The Royal Court International Summer School has just completed its seventh year of developing new international plays with emerging writers and directors from all parts of the world. This year 16 different countries were represented in an intensive workshop with Royal Court practitioners in the Theatre Upstairs and new writing projects are currently underway in many different parts of the world.

In October 1993 the Royal Court began an exciting dialogue with theatre practitioners in the new Germany when a series of readings of new German plays was presented in the Theatre Upstairs. Last year saw the completion of the first phase of this exchange when five Royal Court writers – Kevin Elyot, David Spencer, Martin Crimp, Meredith Oakes and David Greig – had their work translated and read in the world-famous Deutsches Theater in the former East Berlin. All five writers were able to take part in the 'Woche der Englischen Dramatik' with the support of the British Council, and along with Stephen Daldry joined a lively panel discussing new writing in both countries.

Waiting Room Germany appeared in our second series of readings of new German plays, *New German Voices: Plays from a Changing Country*, in October of this year. This week continued the exchange of work with the Deutsches Theater, and was met with great interest and enthusiasm from the public – the entire series was sold out. In response, one month later, *Waiting Room Germany* receives a production in the Theatre Downstairs.

We are grateful to all those people involved in the Deutsches Theater production who responded so swiftly and so generously to our wish to do the play at the Royal

Court, to Corinna Brocher of Rowohlt Verlag and to the British Council. Finally, we could not have produced *Waiting Room Germany* without the support and commitment of the Goethe-Institut, London. We are particularly grateful to Helga Wilderotter-Ikonomou and Henrike Hawkins of the Programme Department for their tremendous commitment to this project.

Elyse Dodgson, Associate Director

The Goethe-Institut

The Goethe-Institut is an independent, non-profit making organisation which aims to promote the study of the German language abroad and to encourage international cultural co-operation. The Goethe-Institut was founded in 1951 in Munich, where its Head Office is situated. There are 16 language teaching centres in Germany. Worldwide 150 branches of the Goethe-Institut in 70 countries now provide German language courses, teacher training, library and information services, as well as cultural projects and events.

In Britain, apart from the London office founded in 1962, branches of the Goethe-Institut are situated in Manchester, York and Glasgow. The Goethe-Institut London helps to promote British-German contacts and interchange through:

• Seminars, conferences and liaison on contemporary issues relevant to both a German and a British public

• Exhibitions of German (particularly contemporary) art and contacts between artists and art experts

• Support of special music programmes in co-operation with British organisations and festivals

• Readings by German writers and events involving literature experts and publishers

• Support of tours by German theatre and dance companies in Great Britain; support of British theatre groups producing German plays; workshops and contacts in the performing arts

The library of the Goethe-Institut London is one of the largest of the Goethe-Institut libraries worldwide. English translations of the new German plays recently presented at the Royal Court Theatre, as well as other translations and videos on German theatre productions, are available from the library.

Goethe-Institut London, 50 Princes Gate, Exhibition Road, London SW7 2PH Tel: 0171 411 3400 Fax: 0171 581 0974

Cast in alphabetical order

Politician's Private Secretary   MAUREEN BEATTIE
Psychiatrist
Factory Worker
Engineer

Shepherd   FREDA DOWIE
Old Woman from Berlin
Frankfurt Christian Democrat
Old Lady from Weimar

Insurance Man   NEIL DUDGEON
Taxi Driver
Car Mechanic
Dissatisfied Worker
Security Guard
Actor

Writer   BARRY JACKSON
Mayor of Bebra
Chief Executive
Local Reporter

Press Officer   ROBIN SOANS
Mayor of Harzgerode
Professor
Master Painter

directed by Mary Peate
translated by David Tushingham
designed by Stewart Laing
lighting by Johanna Town
sound by Paul Arditti

stage manangement Martin Christopher, John Rhodes
costume supervisor Sam Mealing

First performed at the Royal Court Theatre
9 November 1995

Klaus Pohl (writer)

Klaus Pohl was born in Rothenburg ob der Tauber in 1952, and now lives in New York. He trained at one of Germany's leading drama schools, the Max-Reinhardt-Seminar in Berlin, and has acted in productions by Luc Bondy, Giorgio Strehler, Robert Wilson and many others. He is one of the most performed contemporary German writers. His plays include: Da nahm der himmel auch die Frau, Hunsrück, the opera libretto Mainufer, Das Alte Land which won the Mulheim Playwrights Prize and voted play of the year by Theater Heute in 1985, Der Spiegel (after Gogol), La Balkona Bar, Heisses Geld, Karate billi kehrt Zurück, which as Karate-Billy Comes Home was performed in the Royal Court Theatre Upstairs in 1992. Other plays include: Die schöne Fremde, Selbstmord in Madrid, Manni Ramm, and Zettel. He has just directed the original German production of Waiting Room Germany at the Deutsches Theater Berlin which opened on 28th October this year. Several other productions of the same play are planned by different theatres throughout Germany.

Paul Arditti (sound designer)

For the Royal Court: Pale Horse, Rat in the Skull (Royal Court Classics), The Steward of Christendom (and Out of Joint), Not a Game for Boys, Mojo, Simpatico, The Strip, Uganda, The Knocky, Blasted, Peaches, The Editing Process, Babies, Some Voices, Thyestes, My Night With Reg, The Kitchen, The Madness of Esme and Shaz, Hammett's Apprentice, Hysteria, Live Like Pigs, Search and Destroy.
Other theatre sound design includes: The Threepenny Opera (Donmar Warehouse); Hamlet (Gielgud); Piaf (Piccadilly); St Joan.(Strand & Sydney Opera House); The Winters Tale, Cymbeline, The Tempest, Antony & Cleopatra, The Trackers of Oxyrhynchus (RNT); The Gift of the Gorgon (RSC & Wyndhams); Orpheus Descending (Theatre Royal Haymarket & Broadway); A Streetcar Named Desire (Bristol Old Vic); Tartuffe, The Winters Tale (Manchester Royal Exchange); The Wild Duck (Phoenix); Henry IV, The Ride Down Mount Morgan (Wyndhams); Born Again (Chichester); Three Sisters, Matador (Queens); Twelfth Night, The Rose Tatoo (Playhouse); Two Gentlemen of Verona, Beckett, Cyrano de Bergerac (Theatre Royal Haymarket); Travesties (Savoy); Four Baboons Adoring the Sun (Lincoln Center, 1992 Drama Desk Award).
Opera includes: Arianna, Gawain (ROH).
TV includes: The Camomile Lawn.

Maureen Beattie

Born in Bundorran, County Donegal. daughter of Scottish comedian Johnny Beattie. Theatre includes: The Merry Wives of Windsor (RNT); The Man Who Came To Dinner, Mary and Lizzie, The Constant Couple, The Man of Mode, Macbeth (RSC); The Taming of the Shrew (Crucible Sheffield); Innes de Castro (Riverside); Tartuffe (Watford); The Secret Rapture (Northern Stage Co.); Lady Chatterly's Lover (Coventry); Othello (Lyric Hammersmith); Daisy Pulls it Of (Globe); Detective Story (Royal Exchange Manchester); What Every Woman Knows (Scottish Theatre Co.); Marie of Scotland (Edinburgh Festival); The Chinese Wolf (Bush Theatre); Who's Left? (Tron Glasgow); Hard to Get (Traverse Edinburgh); As You Like It, The Playboy of the Western World , The Cherry Orchard (Royal Lyceum Edinburgh). Television includes: The Lost Tribe, The Daftie, The Donegals, The People v Scott, Taggart, Hard to Get, Changes, The Campbells, Truckers, City Lights, The Bill, Casualty, The Long Roads (with her sister Louise Beattie), All Night Long, Ruffian Hearts.

Freda Dowie

Theatre includes: The Maids (Glasgow Citizens); The Buried Man (Library Manchester); Electra (Edinburgh & Greenwich); Casandra (Stratford East); Antigone, Tartuffe, Brunel (Greenwich); I Learned in Ipswich How to Posion Flowers, Within the Fortress (Wolsey, Ipswich); Triumph of Death (Birmingham Rep); The Belle of Amhurst (Theatre Royal Bath & Mercury Colchester); The Dresser (Queens Theatre Hornchurch). One of the original ten actors in Peter Brook's Theatre of Cruelty experiment.
Television includes: Sophia and Constance, Sherlock Holmes, Poirot, Golden Eye, Oranges Are Not The Only Fruit, Kinsey, Thacker, Stay Lucky III, Heartbeat, Boon, Middlemarch, Crime Story, Moving Story, Common As Muck, Our Friends in the North. In Suspicious.
Film: The Omen, Murder by Decree, Scandalous, Distant Voices Still Lives, The Monk, A Life in Death, The Black Crow, Butterfly Kiss.

Neil Dudgeon

For the Royal Court: Shirley, Road, No One Sees the Video, Talking in Tongues.
Other theatre includes: The Importance of Being Earnest, Richard II (Royal Exchange Manchester); Crackwalker (Gate Theatre); Miss Julie (Oldham Coliseum); The Next Best Thing (Nuffield); The Daughter-in-law (Bristol Old Vic); Colliers Friday Night (Greenwich); Yerma, School for Wives (RNT); The Changeling, The School for Scandal (Cambridge Theatre Co & tour); Weekly Rep (Frinton).
Television includes: Road, London's Burning, Piece of Cake, Saracen, Texc, Lovejoy, Night Voice, Casualty, The Bill, Resnick, Between the Lines, Nice Town, Sharpes Eagles, A Touch of Frost, Fatherland, Common as Muck, The All New Alexi Sayle Show, Out of the Blue, Inspector Morse.

Film imcludes: Prick Up Your Ears, Red King White Knight, Fools of Fortune, Revolver, Crossing the Border.

Stewart Laing (designer)

Theatre includes: Venus and Adonis (ATC); War Plays (RSC); The Blue Ball (RNT); Alls Well That Ends Well (New York Shakespeare Festival).
Opera includes: L'Augelino Belle Verde (Battingano); Fidelio (Scottish Opera); Luisa Miller (Opera North and Royal Opera House).
As director and designer: The Homosexual or The Difficulty of Expressing Oneself (Tramway Glasgow); The Father, The She Wolf (Citizens Theatre Glasgow); La Boheme (Scottish Opera-Go-Round); Brainy (C.C.A Glasgow).

Barry Jackson

For the Royal Court: Kelly's Eye.
Theatre includes: The Barber of Seville (Watford); Mice and Men, 'Ere We Go (Crucible); Jumpers (Exchange); Aunt Mary (Donmar Warehouse); Great White Hope (Tricycle); Landmarks (Lyric Studio); The Alchemist (Chichester); Bofors Gun (Hampstead); Caligula (Pheonix); Peace in Our Time (Tour); The Entertainer (Tour).
Television includes: Ellington, Peak Practice, Wycliffe, Heartbeat, Minder, The Chief, A Touch of Frost, Kinsey, Growing Rich, Bergerac, Blore M.P. All Creatures Great and Small, The Act, Hard Cases, Fortunes of War, 1914 All Out, The Great Paperchase, Them and Us, Vicar of Stiffkey, Androcles and the Lion, Pride of Our Alley, Horace, Chains, Cribb, The Crucible, Churchill and the Generals.
Film includes: Mr Love, The Shooting Party, The Bunker, The Luck of Barry Lyndon, Raging Moon, Ryan's Daughter, Diamonds on Wheels, Alfred the Great, Bofors Gun, Aces High.

Mary Peate (director)

For the Royal Court: Arts Council Trainee Director 1992-1994; Oleanna (and Duke of York's); Hammett's Apprentice, The Treatment (Assistant Director). Readings and workshops include: Waiting Room Germany, Cigarettes and Moby Dick, The Distance of You, The Whisper of Angels' Wings.
Theatre includes: Grave Dancer (Finborough); Picnic and Guernica (Gate).
Joint Artistic Director of the Finborough Theatre 1991-1992. Assistant Director at the Gate Theatre, Notting Hill 1990-1991.

Robin Soans

For the Royal Court: Star-Gazy Pie and Sauerkraut, Three Birds Alighting on a Field (1991 & 1992), Etta Jenks, Bed of Roses (also Bush & tour).
Other theatre includes: Volpone (RNT); Raising Fires (Bush); The Country Wife, The Venetian Twins, Murder in the Cathedral (RSC); Walpurgis Night, Gringo Planet (Gate); Germinal, Berlin Days – Hollywood Nights (The Place & tour); Bet Noir (Young Vic); Fashion (Leicester Haymarket); Thatcher's Women (Tricycle & tour); The Rivals (Nottingham Playhouse); A Prick Song for the New Levianthan (Old Red Lion); The Shaming of Bright Millar (Contact Manchester); Queer Fish (BAC); The Worlds, Hamlet,Woyzec, Chobham Amour (Half Moon); Ubu Roi (Jeanetta Cochrane); The Strongest Man in the World. Television includes: Casualty, The Marshall and the Mad-woman, Inspector Alleyn, Anna Lee, Lovejoy, The Specials, This Land of England, The Last Place on Earth, The Chelworth Inheritance, Bergerac, Lord Peter Wimsey, The Bill.
Films include: Comrades, Absolution, The Patricia Neal Story, Hidden City, Blue Juice, Clockwork Mice.

Johanna Town (lighting designer)

For the Royal Court: Pale Horse, The Steward of Christendom (and Out of Joint), Ashes and Sand, The Editing Process, Peaches, Babies, The Kitchen, Search and Destroy, Women Laughing, Faith Healer.
Other theatre lighting design includes: Three Sisters, Road (Out of Joint); Disappeared (Leicester Haymarket & tour); The Lodger (Royal Exchange & Hampstead); Richard II, Street Captives (Royal Exchange); Stiff Stuff (Library Theatre Manchester); Soldiers (CO Producers); Trafford Tanzi (London Bubble); Salvation, The Snow Orchid (London Gay Theatre); The Set-Up, Crackwalker (Gate Theatre); Josephine (BAC); Celestina (ATC); Beautiful Thing (Bush, Donmar, Duke of York's); over 20 designs for Liverpool Playhouse including Macbeth, The Beaux Stratagem, Madame Mao.
Opera includes: The Marriage of Figaro, Eugene Onegin, The Abduction from the Seraglio, The Merry Widow (Opera 80); The Human Voice, Perfect Swine (MTM); The Posion Chalice, The Magic Flute, La Traviata (MTL at the Donmsr and in Hamburg); Otello (Opera Du Nice).
Currently Chief Electrician at the Royal Court.

David Tushingham (translator)

David Tushingham edits LIVE, a polemical review of the performing arts published by Methuen. He previously spent five years as Dramaturg of the Deutsches Theater Schauspiel-haus in Hamburg. He has translated three other plays by Klaus Pohl: Karate-Billy Comes Home, Perfect Stranger and Suicide in Madrid.

The English Stage Company at the Royal Court

The English Stage Company was formed to bring serious writing back to the stage. The Court's first Artistic Director, George Devine, wanted to create a vital and popular theatre. He encouraged new writing that explored subjects drawn from contemporary life as well as pursuing European plays and forgotten classics. When John Osborne's *Look Back in Anger* was first produced in 1956, it forced British theatre into the modern age. But, the Court was much more than a home for 'Angry Young Men' illustrated by a repertoire that stretched from Brecht to Ionesco, by way of J P Sartre, Marguerite Duras, Wedekind and Beckett.

The ambition to discover new work which was challenging, innovative and also of the highest quality became the fulcrum of the Company's policy. Early Court writers included Arnold Wesker, John Arden, David Storey, Ann Jellicoe, N F Simpson and Edward Bond. They were followed by a generation of writers led by David Hare and Howard Brenton, and in more recent years, celebrated house writers have included Caryl Churchill, Timberlake Wertenbaker, Robert Holman and Jim Cartwright. Many of their plays are now regarded as modern classics.

In line with the policy of nurturing new writing, the Theatre Upstairs has mainly been seen as a place for exploration and experiment, where writers learn and develop their skills. Anne Devlin, Andrea Dunbar, Sarah Daniels, Jim Cartwright, Clare McIntyre, Winsome Pinnock, and more recently Martin Crimp and Phyllis Nagy have benefited from this process. Theatre Upstairs productions have regularly transferred to the Theatre Downstairs, as with Ariel Dorfman's *Death and the Maiden*, and this autumn Sebastian Barry's *The Steward of Christendom*, a co-production with *Out of Joint*. This was part of a major season of plays by writers new to the Royal Court, many of them first plays, produced in association with the Royal National Theatre Studio with sponsorship from the Jerwood Foundation. The writers included Joe Penhall, Nick Grosso, Judy Upton, Sarah Kane, Michael Wynne, Judith Johnson and James Stock.

1992-1995 were record-breaking years at the box-office with capacity houses for productions of *Faith Healer, Death and the Maiden, Six Degrees of Separation, King Lear, Oleanna, Hysteria, Cavalcaders, The Kitchen, The Queen and I, The Libertine, Simpatico* and *Mojo*.

Death and the Maiden and *Six Degrees of Separation* won the Olivier Award for Best Play in 1992 and 1993 respectively. *Hysteria* won 1994's Olivier Award for Best Comedy, and also the Writers' Guild Award for Best West

End Play. *My Night with Reg* won the 1994 Writers' Guild Award for Best Fringe Play, the Evening Standard Award for Best Comedy, and Best Comedy in this year's Olivier Awards. Jonathan Harvey won the 1994 Evening Standard Drama Award for Most Promising Playwright, for *Babies*. Sebastian Barry won the 1995 Writers' Guild Award for Best Fringe Play for *The Steward of Christendom*, Jez Butterworth was named *New Writer of the Year* for *Mojo* by the Writers' Guild and Phyllis Nagy won the Writers' Guild Award for Best Regional Play for *Disappeared*. The Royal Court has just been awarded the *1995 Prudential Award for Excellence and Innovation in Theatre.*

After nearly four decades, the Royal Court's aims remain consistent with those established by George Devine. The Royal Court Theatre is still a major focus in the country for the production of new work. Scores of plays first seen in Sloane Square are now part of the national and international dramatic repertoire.

The Royal Court Theatre is financially assisted by the Royal Borough of Kensington and Chelsea.

Recipient of a grant from the Theatre Restoration Fund and from the Foundation for Sport & the Arts.

The Royal Court's Play Development Programme is funded by the Audrey Skirball-Kenis Theatre. This theatre has the support of the Thames Television Writers' Scheme sponsored and administered by Thames Television.

The Royal Court Registered Charity number 231242

WAITING ROOM GERMANY

A Note on the Text

Waiting Room Germany is unusually open in form. There is no prescribed cast or order of speeches. It can be performed by one actor, by a cast of thirty, or any number of combinations in between. All the characters are real people speaking their own words, shaped into speeches by the author from personal interviews. The full text is too long to be performed in a single evening.

The present edition has been published to coincide with the production at the Royal Court Theatre, London, in November 1995, and aims to reproduce the text used on this occasion. Anyone planning a production of their own may wish to consult a fuller version, available in an English translation from A.P. Watt Ltd, 20 John Street, London WC1N 2DL, or in the original German from Rowholt Theater Verlag, Hamburger Strasse 17, 21462 Reinbeck, Germany.

David Tushingham

Characters:

Insurance Man
Press Officer
Politician's Private Secretary
Writer
Taxi Driver
Psychiatrist
Old Woman from Berlin
Mayor of Bebra, a town in West Germany
Mayor of Harzgerode, a town in East Germany
Factory Worker
Professor
Car Mechanic
Engineer
Chief Executive
Frankfurt Christian Democrat
Disatisfied Worker
Local Reporter
Old Lady from Weimar
Security Guard
Master Painter
Actor

Insurance Man

The first time
oh God
the first time I went across
I'm driving across there
get to the border
the wall was down
and the *Volkspolizei* were giving everyone such a friendly wave
I just had to stop
and tell one of them
I told him:
'I'm going to say something now
which isn't very pleasant
you weren't the one who wouldn't let me go the last time
but you're part of the same system
so I'm telling you
if I had my way now
I'd kick your teeth in.'

Press Officer

One has to ask whether it's really right
that we've basically taken a different system
and forced it on these people.
I don't know how the *Wessis* would have reacted
whether they would have been able to show as much
let's call it endurance
as some of the *Ossis* have had to have.
It's as if the Japanese had invaded West Germany and
    announced
from tomorrow you are under Japanese law
everything you have been doing up until now is irrelevant
whether it's traffic regulations or tax law
even the constitution
forget it!
From tomorrow everything's Japanese!

Politician's Private Secretary

For me more or less everything's changed.
Before I was an academic
I used to sit here at my desk
quietly writing my dissertation
articles books and stuff.
The sort of thing that academics do:
international criminal and civil law.
And I had a husband
and so on and so forth
and we all lived here together
the three of us.
You've got to understand that
the DDR was coming to an end.
Something else was on its way
you could see
it was all going down the drain
with things like banning *Sputnik* magazine.
Then when he left us
at the end of 87
beginning of 88
I really felt:
society's fucked
my relationship's fucked
everything's fucked!
So.
When I told people
we wouldn't make it to the next century
everyone laughed at me.
But there were signs everywhere that things were coming to a
    head.
Then the butter crisis happened
and loads more people left.
Buildings started emptying around you:
another one gone here, another empty window there.
You could feel it in the air:
the End is nigh.
Like you can tell a storm's coming
because the flies keep so close to the ground.
Well.
I flipped.
Everything was suddenly going so fast
one thing being replaced by another
then finally everyone breathed a massive sigh of relief.
We thought a new era was going to begin.

the new DDR!
We were all very shaken by it:
I was ill for three months with a sweat gland abcess
sitting round with icepacks under my arm the whole time
I could only walk like this.
I told people my body was purging itself of socialism.
Everything seemed to be festering away.
It was like: you knew it was all going to come crashing apart
but you had no idea where the break was going to come
and which direction it would take you.
What did come was a huge disappointment.
I didn't want to be part of West Germany.
It was unrecognizable.
Suddenly they were only taking on Westerners:
we were pushed aside overnight.
From planned economy to market economy – bang.
It might work with the economy. But not with people.
The quick fix had irreversible consequences for them.
On 3rd October my job was terminated.
They got rid of me.
Herr Reckers came over from the Chancellor's office
we got certificates
with heartfelt thanks for your contribution to German unity
shake hands *auf Wiedersehen*
hello unemployment.
It was a huge stroke of luck
that I managed to find something else.
What saved me was having such a big gob.
So.
I applied to the regional government in Brandenburg
and they took me on and found me a job.
It would never have happened
if I hadn't had a doctorate.
At that level they normally only take people from the West.
And now I'm Stolpe's Private Secretary.
I do everything for him
and anything Eastern is my job
when people ring up saying they'll hang themselves
or set themselves on fire.
Then we've got to <u>do</u> something.
They ring me saying things like:
'If you lot don't do this and that
I'm gonna hang myself right on your doorstep.'
Desperate people.
I get a lot of them.
I make sure I go and see them.

The big problem is that
for the DDR population, which still exists here -
that's the amazing thing:
they've managed to emigrate without going anywhere -
the laws are all different
the punishments, the rules have changed
and none of the poor buggers can see their way through it.
So.
If you're anything like me
I mean I can't face seeing them all cry
then I go and sort it out for them.
And of course the word gets round.
That's what I try to explain to all these officials
who've come over from the West
who don't understand this at all!
They have no idea what's going on here!
They simply don't appreciate the scale of the problem!
The people just get in their way!
I end up shouting at them, telling them
there ought to be a sign up here:
YOU ARE PAID BY LOCAL PEOPLE ALL DAY LONG!
And when those people need you
it's your job to fucking well be there for them!
Not too busy shunting a load of forms
from one side of your desk to the other.
Because that's bollocks!
So.
Two different worlds are colliding head on there.
There was one bloke rang up for example.
Owned a haulage firm quite near here, just outside Berlin.
And this bloke explained
he owned a piece of land
- it's all connected to this issue of
Westerners claiming property in the East -
he's got this land
and he's fought it out so that he can keep it
but he's got this haulage business -
he has horses -
and now he needs to build a stable for them on his property.
But because everything's new
and everything has to be approved again
he needs planning permission
and because right now that's what everyone needs
there are millions of applications piling up
and at the moment there's an 18 month wait
for an application to get processed.

Now the other guy, the *Wessi*,
who still wants the land back
just won't leave him alone.
So.
He's been poisoning the dogs, poisoning the animals
trying to get rid of him
and that means:
the bloke has to have a stable for his horses and his animals
    right now
and if he doesn't get one, then the animals will all be dead
and he won't need a stable any more.
He'll be ruined.
So.
What do you do?
I've got him on the other end of the phone in floods of tears:
'the Prime Minister is my only hope,' he's saying.
That's what they all want:
a few words with the king as it were
but they don't get to speak to the king
because I'm there.
And I ring his local council Chief Executive's office.
You see that's the great advantage
of you doing all the groundwork:
you know everyone.
So I can call the Chief Executive
and say: 'Burkhard. Come on. Stop sitting on the fence!
There's a man in tears here.
Now listen. Find his planning application -
now I know you're not allowed to do this –
but stick it on top of the pile and get it approved quick.
Or else the previous owner is going to kill all his animals.'
'So what's he ringing you for?'
And I say: 'Yes, I wonder.
Probably because you told him to go to the back of the queue.
I know what you're like!'
And then of course I say the Prime Minister has asked specially!
In fact he doesn't know the slightest thing about it.
But I do a bit of the old Politburo
making him personally responsible
calling him *du* all the time
and in the East that still works like magic.
And then I had a woman who was really at her wits' end.
Her daughter had been sleeping around.
She'd picked up a gang of Russians and was hanging about with
    them
in their barracks getting up to all sorts

14 or 15 she was
she'd dropped out
hadn't been to school for over a year.
The mother was quite desperate.
'You know something,' she told me.
'I'm gonna get a can of petrol
and set myself on fire right outside the Prime Minister's office.'
Now there are two reasons you don't want this to happen:
(a) because it's a political issue
people setting fire to themselves outside government offices
and (b) because it is a shame about the woman.

Insurance Man

Plauen, yes:
it's going back a while now
going back
well four years ago
it was just after the wall came down
I went over
to get things established.
One result of opening the border
was that the whole Western health insurance system
came in.
And just then
every insurance company was making a big effort -
it was a fiercely contested market.
Anyway, Plauen.
It was very nice at the beginning.
Of course it meant a lot of hard work
and I wasn't exactly popular
I was the ultimate *Wessi*!
First in in the morning and last to leave.
I used to make them twitch
they would all stand to attention
when I came into the room.
Because I told them:
There's one thing I don't like -
I made it very plain -
this
this er
this vocabulary
they would always come out with
brigades and er
what was it they used to say
I told them:
'We'll have none of that here!
We're in the West now
and we're going to work in a western way.
I'm not your brigadier
and I won't let myself be called that.
We are all employees
and I am the most senior employee' -
sometimes a highly dubious privilege!
My main priority was
not to leave a disaster behind me.
That when the time came for me
to leave Plauen

I could hand it over
in full working order – and it would stay working.
They'll never forget me for that!
And what's happened since
that I'm particularly pleased about
which is a real positive development
is that the Plauen branch
is now run by local people:
they've come that far in this short time.
Two women run it.
They're the managers!
One of them, one of my appointees, is the deputy,
and the other one who's taken it over now
is a particularly intelligent woman
who I always used to have right at the front
where we had our information centre
and I put her there
because she seemed particularly attractive.
She was dark and very striking
and she used to say hello to everyone who came in,
this smart lady at the reception desk,
who is now the manager.
I had to appoint 27 people
together with a certain Herr Schal from Hof
and I picked 26 women
that was my contribution to German reunification:
women only.
The regional office gave me a warning
I dealt with that in one sentence:
What we want are customers
and that depends to a large extent on outward appearances
Women are better-looking than men!
Of course you need to have at least one token man
but I'd already got him.
'That's me!
The token man.'
To begin with we went round the factories
I had to do most of the business myself
visiting companies
they would take one look at my suit and briefcase
and send me straight to the boss
then it all depends
on how you handle the meeting
I say you've got to be able to work with your voice -
it has to resonate
it also needs a comic touch occasionally

they've got to be able to hear: that's alive!
it has to be alive
not just dripping out of your mouth.
The whole occasion
has to be a positive experience.
Another thing I told them -
they couldn't care less
I did -
was the importance
of presentation.
If you give someone
a business card
it has to be clean
not dog-eared
it has to make a mark.
Otherwise the client'll think you're a fool!
And that also means the building has to be clean and tidy.
What always bothered me most
was their toilets.
The pissoir – it was one of the stupidest things.
I told them: I get the impression
everyone misses when they go for a pee.
What actually caused it -
I was never one to mince my words -
what caused it was the flush
whenever you pressed it down – pfffft! -
some of it always squirted out
and the drips
missed the pissoir and landed on the floor.
The pressure was too high.
In the pipes.
So I said: let's lower the pressure
So that's what I did
we ripped out all the old plumbing
and had Western plumbing put in everywhere.
So that the pressure was right.
Some things you've got to say to people straight out.
Mm. No matter how unpleasant or embarrassing. Mm.
One woman used to stink of sweat.
Take more showers.
No.
No-no.
I didn't tell her: You should take more showers.
I said: you should pay more attention to personal hygiene.
I said it to her alone.
Not in front of all the others.

12

That's the stupidest thing you could possibly do.
Forget that.
Not in front of everyone else.
I had my own office.
That helped.
I got her in and said it to her.
It's purely a question of cultivating good habits.
Personal hygiene consists of showering regularly, washing
    regularly
and not just your face! but all the other embarrassing bits too.
If I change my shirt every day the smell of sweat in my clothes
can never be very strong even if I don't wash very regularly!
But if I wear the same shirt three days a week –
then the smell starts to sink in and broadcast itself
and that reflects badly on the company.
I explained to her,
that if you went up to the cash desk it didn't seem to smell very
    nice.
And then the lady said she understood.
Most of them would come to see me in my office.
Mm! It smells of the West. They used to say.
They wanted to come inside.
I would be wearing cologne and that smelt nice,
it created a pleasant atmosphere.
Wherever I went there was always a little bit of a cloud hanging
    around me.
And I made it quite clear to the people in Plauen:
what I do, anyone else can do too.
As long as they're prepared to make the effort.
It all depends on the effort you put in.
People there didn't care about what they were doing.
You'd turn up somewhere and the receptionists would all be
    filing their nails.
Or talking amongst themselves.
The phone would ring and I'd have to ask them to answer it.
They'd say: if they really want something they'll try again!
It was mad!
I sent one of the staff over to the bank.
I told her to fetch the statements.
I thought she was never coming back.
I could have hopped there and back in that time!
I waited an hour! An hour and a half, two hours!
I needed the statements, I wanted to see how things were doing
and I couldn't leave the office before I'd done the returns.
I was responsible for almost all the work outside the branch
and I had people to visit.

13

I couldn't waste my time just sitting around on my backside.
I looked all over the place for her.
I thought she was never coming back.
By then it's almost noon.
And she turns up with a new haircut!
Yes, she'd been to the hairdressers.
Yes, she'd always been in her work time before.
Well, your hair grows while you're working doesn't it?
That was the answer I got.
That was the difference in attitudes.
They would grumble that I was always putting in 1000%.
'Does the whole place belong to you?'
They couldn't understand that.
'You're only the brigadier.'
And I said. 'I am not a brigadier, I am the branch manager.'
They thought it was a collective
the society was some sort of collective
that's the way they saw it.
They used to, that thinking's gone now.
But at the beginning you had to explain all that.
Now it's more like here.
It's all fitting into place now.

Writer

They'd started this cadet school
two months before Hungary
and they were looking for people
who were good at sport as well as academically and politically -
they were intended to become the army élite
and would be trained there.
I was eleven.
My father sent for me while I was playing football
and told me: this is something
you ought to think about
whether you want to do it or not.
You'll be taught how to shoot
you'll be taught how to ride a horse
you'll be taught how to ride a motorbike
you'll be taught everything you need for the army
and you'll have one holiday a year -
and you'll have to appear before a panel
who will give you sporting and academic tests.
But only if that's what you want!
I agreed on the spot!
And he told me: think about it for a few days
don't say yes straight away!
My mother didn't interfere.
So I spent a couple of days thinking about it
and all I could feel was fear that I might not be one
of these 330 superhumans.
A lot of them dropped out though.
The physical tests were quite tough.
I could do them
I was very fit
and I went along quite happily.
Only: 5 days
before I went I knew
I was making the biggest mistake of my life
5 days before
I went to the theatre
I went to the theatre for the first time
and saw *A Doll's House*
at the Volksbühne in the Luxemburgplatz.
It was *A Doll's House*
I sat there with my mother
and when Nora leaves -
I identified her with my mother -
when Nora suddenly leaves

slamming the door behind her
I had tears rolling down my face and I didn't know why.
And then it occurred to me: everyone's heart has two sides.
One side of you wants to rush off and be an anarchist
and the other side, the other side of your heart, wants to feel
    safe.
And anyone who says their heart has only one of these sides
either the anarchist side
or the other side which wants to stay at home
is lying!
So when Nora slammed the door behind her
I thought:
why aren't I allowed to stay with my family
instead of going to cadet school?
I went anyway.
They gave you a track suit
and two days later you got a uniform
just like the Army ones
they were made to measure.
I was 4' 10'
and that looks really wierd
one of those uniforms on a little kid.
The things used to itch like hell.
It was like a prison
there were watchtowers all around
a very high wall
and guards in all the towers
they let us out once
but only
in groups of four
for two hours
on Sunday.
There were combat exercises
alert: American spies in the area near Weissenfels!
And we all had to rush off and find them.
For about a year and a half it was OK.
Then I wrote to my parents:
I want to be a writer.
What am I doing here?
My father wrote back:
people don't become writers because that's what they've been
    trained for
they do it because they know about life -
I've still got that letter -
and he sent me biographical details
of some famous writers

16

and they were Hemingway,
Faulkner and Maxim Gorky.
They'd been through the school of life.
Graduated from the university of life.
There was no way out.
So then I claimed to be an enemy of the state!
Nothing happened
none of the bastards believed me
I told everyone!
Told them: socialism stinks!
No reaction.
I would make speeches after lights out
about all sorts of things
Capitalism is better!
Adolf Hitler was right!
So was the Catholic Church!
I wanted to break every tabu possible.
My friends just pissed themselves laughing.
They knew why I was doing it all.
Shut up, they said,
let us get some sleep.
The school was closed down in June 1960.
Then the wall came
August 61
it was the holidays
and everyone was talking about how something had to be done
it was always in the paper:
we will no longer tolerate others poaching our workforce
and there was going to be some sort of reaction
but no-one really thought everything would be closed off.
On 13th August I woke up about 11 o'clock
about 11 o'clock my mother came running through the flat
      shouting:
At last! At last!
At last what? I asked
At last we've finally shut the door.
I got on the S-Bahn and went to the station at Friedrichstrasse
the place was full of farmers
from the outskirts of Berlin
who wanted to get out that weekend.
They'd got there
to find everything shut
and they were just sitting there with their suitcases
they'd sold everything they had
on the black market
livestock and furniture

and now they knew they were going to have to go back!
They knew they couldn't buy their things back
they couldn't get across either
so they just sat there crying.
I'll never forget that
swarms of people from Friedrichstrasse to the Brandenburg
    Gate.
And they'd understood instinctively
that they were being shut in.
The intellectuals hadn't!
But the farmers had!
They'd come a day too late
but they'd felt it.
Then there was 68.
Prague.
When Sanda and I came back from the coast
on 22nd August 1968
we thought we'd arrive at Friedrichshagen station
and find the whole city at boiling point.
For the first time one socialist country was invading another
and that was a situation where it was really going to go off.
But there was nothing.
Absolute quiet.
The streets were empty.
Public awareness had died.
I fell in love once with a music teacher at school.
She had thick thighs
and used to sit there looking really unhappy.
Now if I write
about my fat music teacher
and it accidentally gets published
then you bastards will all say:
now he's going all conventional so he'll get published
now he's not a dissident any more.
But because I'm a writer I have to write about it
regardless
of whether it's dissident or conventional!
Honecker's stupidity is not the stuff of literature
nor is defining your position towards the state!
If you'd asked Kafka to define his position vis-à-vis the
    Habsburg monarchy
he'd have polished it off in a diary entry.
It's in there:
a.m. swimming lesson
p.m. outbreak of World War I.
Germany is the only place where it's like this

18

where writers are seen as alternative priests
who are going to tell you what's good, what's right.
That's why
I've kept my mouth shut
since the wall's been opened.
What can I say about it?
It's one subject
where I prefer
to maintain a deafening
deafening
silence.

Taxi Driver

I came over in 1976
76 yeah
the rest of the family were brought across
my father
had been in prison
in Bautzen
and was released
well bought out
in 76.
We applied for exit visas
and followed him.
I was 17 then.
My father was inside for three and a half years
he couldn't handle this schizophrenic situation in the East
any longer.
He'd got to be quite high up
and he'd had to run with the wolves
and a time came when he didn't want to any more.
He'd stayed over in the West
he'd been allowed to travel
and they went and brought him back again
and locked him up
for contacting enemies of the state.
They kept him in Hohenschönhausen for 18 months
on remand
then sent him to Bautzen,
when I was 13.
I was allowed to visit him once.
By then I was 15
it was a meeting of very few words.
When they put him inside
my reaction was angry and defiant
I'd always been good at school
but I went steadily downhill after that
I was in the 2nd year.
I got into arguments with teachers
and
well
things just went on from there.
Then I had to leave for the West.
Even though in the meantime
my life had changed a great deal.
I had a girlfriend.
I was in love

and I didn't want to leave any more.
I wanted to stay there.
In the DDR.
But I was 17
I wasn't an adult
and I had to go
I had no choice!
We were told to pack our bags
it all had to be done in 24 hours.
I said goodbye the day before.
Then we travelled out through Friedrichstrasse.
They wouldn't let us past the checkpoint
till we'd missed our train.
Then I started an apprenticeship
in Munich as a car mechanic.
I thought that would interest me
fiddling around with cars and stuff.
But I wasn't happy at all
I just kept crying all the time
suddenly bursting into tears
because I was so homesick
I couldn't understand what was going on.
I had huge rows with my father
we ripped lumps out of each other.
I told him: I've got to go back.
I dropped out of the course
and went back to Berlin.
I managed to visit my girlfriend a few times
I could get across to see her
until I was 18.
As soon as I was 18
I wasn't allowed over any more.
There was no reason.
They don't give you a reason.
It's perverse.
I wasn't allowed in! End of story!
By that time we'd got engaged in Prague and everything.
But they wouldn't let me back in.
Eventually she broke off the relationship
under pressure from her father
he was under pressure from the State Security.
He was involved in training young people
so they told him if he wasn't even able
to bring up his own daughter properly
and get her to change her ways
then he was hardly in a position

21

to instruct young citizens of the DDR in the correct way of life.
So I was all alone in West Berlin.
We wrote each other over 200 letters.
I've still got most of them.
Then the time came when I told myself:
you've got to forget the whole fucking East.
That's when I started taking drugs
I
I drifted off -
never finished the apprenticeship.
They weren't just soft drugs either.
Really odd things happened to me.
Difficult.
It was the loneliness.
I had a series of brief flings
but there was never any love.
I'd turned her into a goddess
and that makes it hard to find anyone new...
I don't remember much about what happened then.
Over the years I kept on trying
to reestablish contact with her
because I felt there was still something there
something I needed to sort out.
I just wanted to see her again
but she never wanted to.
Eventually she did reply
we met up
and it was very nice
we felt really close
even though we'd not seen each other for such a long time
there was a little bit of love left there after all.
Some disappointment too
because
well I realised I didn't find her at all attractive.
That was a bit of a relief too to be honest.
We hadn't seen each other for 13 years.
For me it was tremendously important
that they opened the wall again.
She never got married.
She had a kid some time
with some bloke who'd always fancied her.
I don't see her any more,
sadly.
She lives with a bloke I used to know
an old adversary
he's jealous, he doesn't like her seeing me

because there's still a little bit of love left in her too.
I can't call her.
I can't go round.
She doesn't want me to.
Maybe I was cheated out of part of my life
but I've had other chances
I passed my *Abitur*
and became a student again.
I've been driving a taxi for the last 6 and a half years
part-time to start with
I began a while back studying art history and ethnology
and this was a way of paying for it
I've not finished it yet -
that's another of these things
not getting that finished -
But I'm still registered for
art history and ethnology:
restoring old railway monuments.
I've been doing it nine years now.
Somehow I don't think it'll ever get finished.

Psychiatrist

We'd be told: The oppressed may now speak
and it would be this petty little voice booming into a microphone
'THIS IS THE DDR'
that sort of thing has always been a real German speciality
these divisive concepts
We were always told
that the West was full of capitalists
and the capitalists were shit
and everything that we were guilty of in the recent past
- thank Christ – was their fault
and that meant Hitler, the Nazis and all this German filth wasn't
    so bad
because it didn't have anything to do with us any more.
And since
and since
since then something much better had come our way
and that was
this red fascism
this was an attitude that was forced on you:
that
that
you thought capitalism was the worst thing ever.
I still keep coming up against
this simplistic equation of
capitalism equals imperialism equals
fascism equals concentration camps
in other words
if you're not a capitalist then you can't be an
imperialist and therefore not a fascist or
anything
but if you actually look
at how it all happened
Russia
could not have been more imperialist
while Hitler was around
and then they carried on doing it for another 40 years!
it wasn't until 49 that they really got started!
The redder than red communists
the ones who came back from Moscow
all had this thing
fixed in their skulls about
ideals of human advancement in the modern age
something like that.
Whatever, they had some sort of ideal person in mind

and everyone assumed
that that was what you had to be
and if you weren't like that now
then you better become it quick!
And er
eventually I decided I wasn't playing any more
and I said: I don't care about what you think people ought to be
    like
I'm going to go and join those evil capitalists
and do what I want to do!
It meant you were a total outcast
but what the hell.
I'm going to go
where I'm supposed to belong.
I'd just got out of prison
I was still on probation
you can't risk more than that!
and I got away!
And over here
maybe in certain respects it was just like the DDR but
at least you could choose what to do about it
for the first time you could choose
how you wanted to react to what was on offer
you could choose your profession
and how you wanted to do things.
It was entirely up to you
no-one was trying to force you to do a particular job
or whatever!
I'm sure I spent a lot of my time
on thoroughly daft things
but still
it was my own life I was living
You see
when you got out of that cage
that gigantic concentration camp
full of lunatics -
I know what I'm talking about -
And you got out here!
You really could
throw yourself into life
I'm going here now or I'm going there!
Money – amazing!!
I had huge problems with it
for years afterwards
I couldn't handle money
because I hadn't the slightest idea what it was

I didn't realize what it meant
the stuff
you see
I had no real understanding of it.
The money in the East was useless.
It was a joke.
And this sudden feeling
of I can do whatever I like...
it was quite daunting
but ultimately it inspired me
THAT THAT'S ME
FOR THE FIRST TIME
I HAD A REAL LUST FOR LIFE
A HUNGER FOR IT
And not just fear
...and we've all got
a pretty hefty biography behind us
which is all bound up with this point
that the world's been divided so conveniently
with all the pigs over there
and all the good guys here with us
and eventually
you've got to say
I DON'T WANT TO BE YOUR PIG FOREVER
I'D RATHER GO AND LIVE WITH THE PIGS
then at least I'll be left alone.
And
and they say
alright piss off then
and then suddenly they come trotting along wanting a pension
for being so thick in the first place!
That's the Germans for you!
I'm one of the ones who got out
and I got out
under very difficult
circumstances
I
I
I risked MY LIFE!
So just when you think: right, that's finished
along they all come
and it's always:
WE'VE BEEN SO BADLY TREATED!
JUST 'COS WE'RE THE *OSSIS*!
And all that crap
and

and you can only think
you've not nearly been treated badly enough
you cunts
first you should sort out your own mess
your pavements
your FRIDGE!!!!
and keep your mouths shut!
But instead it's the poor *Ossis*
and the SOLIDARITY LEVY
and money
and unemployment
and Nazis
and suddenly the tables have been turned
and the grotesque face!
eh!
which had been hidden all this time
has finally been revealed.
What's going on? Fascism.
That's what's going on!
Right now everything bad is coming
from over there
honestly!
At least for someone like me
where I think: <u>You</u> ought to be paying <u>me</u> a pension!
I can't run away again
that would be the second time!
It stinks when someone tells you:
you can kiss my arse for all I care
I don't give a fuck whether you live or die
and you tell them ok and you leave, you go somewhere else
then five minutes later they turn up and ask can you spare a few
    Marks
simply for being stupid enough to talk such shit for years and
    years.
That's great, that is.
How come they're my neighbours?
I don't want them!
They didn't want me
as their neighbour either.
They didn't want me looking them in the face
they couldn't have cared less what happened to me
if they'd held PUBLIC HANGINGS
those people would have gone and watched
me getting my head chopped off.
They would.
I swear to you.

Old Woman from Berlin

Five years ago is it now?
What! It can't be. Dear me. 5 years – oh my God!
I must say so much has changed.
We've got all these unemployed people
and we can get all these things that we never had before
and everyone can travel wherever they want.
If they've got the money.
I haven't been anywhere.
Nowhere at all.
I can't, I've got a son at home who's sick,
I have to stay at home,
I can only get as far as the cemetery,
I can't leave him on his own any longer.
The reunification has done nothing for me,
no, not for me, nothing.
But my other two sons, they've both done a lot of travelling.
I don't begrudge them it
after all the hard times they've been through.
We were stuck in Berlin in 45.
We'd been evacuated a couple of times, to Wartegau.
A woman with three children for God's sake!
They didn't want us anywhere...
We were stuck here in the cellar and it had all been in vain.
Still, we survived.
I'll never forget the war as long as I live, the things we saw.
1000 years could go by and I'd still not forget.
The dead soldiers piled up in the Friedrichstrasse, this high they
    were!
And standing on top of the house to put out the fire next door –
you won't forget that! The whole city was in flames!
I have to tell you, I have nothing to do with politics.
That's finished as far as I'm concerned.
I'll be 80 in September, I'm taken care of, let's say,
and as long as I still can
I'm going to do what I can for my son and I.
Politics isn't my responsibility any more.
During the war we would go out with the three boys
and dig roots up out of the snow to make coffee.
Indoors everything froze; the ink, the coffee!
The windows just had thin black paper over them
and it was such a cold winter. But we didn't freeze.
My beautiful homeland. That's what I like most.
All of it. The whole of Germany. Especially the Baltic coast;
Rügen, Warnemunde, Heringsdorf. Stockmunde.

The countryside where I come from,
West Prussia, which is now in Poland, that's very beautiful too.
We'd be so happy when the first flowers appeared,
when the heather was in bloom.
There was a wood behind our house
we used to pick blueberries there by the bucketful,
we had everything, wonderful game, it was gorgeous.
Germany was very, very beautiful in those days.
The people had to work so hard, day and night.
It was called Steinow, the village, and it was very poor,
it really was nothing but stones, but so beautiful.
We used to go and fetch Easter water and all those sorts of
    things.
On Easter Day we used to have to get up very early, before the
    sunrise,
and go down to the spring.
The water came out of the ground, you could see it coming out,
icy-cold, beautifully clear and it tasted so good.
We used to put bicarbonate of soda in it;
vinegar, bicarbonate and sugar,
you could go on drinking it till you burst,
my children would have drunk themselves to death on the stuff.
It was lovely. You don't get that any more.
I don't want to complain.
The people were different in those days.
At New Year everybody would call out to each other.
Later it got so bad nobody could laugh any more...

Mayor of Bebra, a town in West Germany

What annoyed me most this morning
was the appointment I had with my dentist
which I'd arranged specially for this morning
had to be cancelled
because my crowns weren't ready.
Now here I am without any crowns on my teeth.
You'll have to excuse me if
er
my lip...
Here we are in front of the Old Town Hall
in Bebra.
It cost about a million Marks to renovate.
And these hens
you can see along the front:
they're made of concrete.
We got them from Thüringen
from an artist in Thüringen
who makes all sorts of concrete animals:
crocodiles, elephants, hens.
Because the Old Town Hall
was originally a farm
we thought it would be fun to have a row of hens here
and a cockerel in front.
To remind people that it was once a farm.
Will you look at that:
someone's knocked the cockerel's comb off.
That's another piece of vandalism.
They're concrete hens, like I said. The hen set!
If you've got a garden give him a call,
he'll deliver.
But the unification! Reunification!
Complete and total reunification!
When the wall came down
the town of Bebra made 1200 Marks' worth of coffee.
We did it in shifts.
People were getting up at four in the morning
to make coffee for all the people coming from the East
coffee
coffee
coffee
coffee
Now there was no way the town could have predicted the
    reunification
and everything has to be budgeted for in advance

so we just didn't have this 1200 Marks' coffee money for the
     reunification!
It's obvious!
Anyhow the Edeka coffee company volunteered
and said we'll put in 1000 Marks and everyone gave a donation.
But the ones
the ones who really made a packet
the supermarkets like Aldi -
they didn't give us a thing!
We were all euphoric about the situation:
the border has gone,
Bebra is slap bang in the middle of Germany,
I'm the Mayor:
things can only get better
with industry coming in and so forth.
Instead the opposite has happened.
The federal authorities have closed their offices down
like customs
and border patrols
there used to be 25 customs officers here
with dogs.
The railway police -
moved to Fulda!
No-one in Bebra believed reunification would ever happen.
Why did I become Mayor of Bebra?
Well
personal reasons partly
Bebra is a place where you can keep an eye on everything
but because you can still keep an eye on everything
there are a lot of demands on your time.
Loads of people make appointments
to come and see me.
The usual problem is people
driving too fast.
Another thing that keeps cropping up is
people not getting on with their neighbours
then for some reason
THE MAYOR AS AN INSTITUTION
is supposed to intervene
because they haven't got the guts to go and talk to the people
     next door
and sort it out between themselves.
Their neighbours don't even know that there's a problem:
that at that very moment neighbour number 1
is sitting in the Mayor's office complaining about neighbour
     number 2.

Nowadays we live in a state
which wants everything minutely ordered and regulated
and these regulations bear no relation to what happens in
    practice.
Everything is regulated
down to the tiniest detail.
I'll give you one example.
Of course there are rules for kindergartens.
But there's a rule for the precise distance
between the hooks for the children's coats.
Because it might be possible
for a flea to jump between them.
They've measured it.
The distance has to be
this is of the top of my head
at least 8 cm.
All this gets written down
and enshrined in law.
Another example!
The State of Hessen
and the town of Bebra
are building a cycle path together.
Building in inverted commas that is.
Because they've been doing it for 15 years now
and the thing still hasn't been built yet.
And why is that?
Because the path runs alongside a national park.
It wouldn't actually enter the protected area.
The edge of the cycle path or the edge of the road
would touch the edge of the protected area.
That's all that would happen: they would touch each other.
But for the conservation authorities
that means: NO!
They've used various arguments:
that the animals would be disturbed
if a cyclist stopped to have a look round.
There are grey herons there.
There was a suggestion that
we put the cycle path on the other side of the road.
Even though there are woods there
and it would mean felling the first rows of trees
and that cyclists coming from Bebra
would have to cross the B27 – a very busy road.
So to stop them from being run over and killed
we were supposed to build an underpass.
That underpass would have cost half a million Marks!

And that's where I said:
'Hang on!
It is simply not on
that the life of a frog or a swarm of mosquitoes
or a grey heron -
never mind merely causing them a disturbance -
is going to cost that kind of money!
I won't allow it!'
So then we had a meeting
with a representative
of the Federal Environmental Protection Authority.
He told us all about the grey herons.
'If a cyclist stops on the cycle path
and a grey heron happens to be there
then the grey heron is going to be disturbed.'
So I told him:
'Right, this is what we'll do,
we'll build a screen all round the park.
It doesn't matter what the cyclists do then
they won't ever see any grey herons.'
And that will be the answer.

Mayor of Harzgerode, a town in East Germany

I was Mayor of Harzgerode
for ten years
between 1980 and 1990.
I stopped on 15th March 1990
I stood down officially
and handed over
all my official duties.
It was all done properly
and initially
after a lot of thought
I decided to distance myself
quite firmly
from all party-political activities.
At that time
I felt very badly let down
by our SED
I have to say that
I'd spent my entire life
doing a great deal for the Party
I was quite aware of what I was doing
and I genuinely supported the ideals
which the Party used to stand for.
I come from a pure working class background
I trained as a carpenter
before changing jobs
that's when I came here to Harzgerode
there was industry here
die-casting it was then
a small company
and the company then chose me to go on a course
and I studied economic management for 5 years.
5 years of evening classes
working during the day and studying at night
and on top of that
in my spare time
I was a musician in a dance band
trumpet
I played.
I was an economist
in the labour department.
Then I was put in charge
of personnel, training and social welfare.
And then well
in 1980

I had to
I was forced to volunteer
it was well-known
the Party didn't let you discuss these things
the regional First Secretary came along
together with the Council Leader for the area
and they didn't beat about the bush.
Look, Manfred, Comrade,
we expect you etcetera etcetera
will take over as Mayor on 1st October
and if you have any objections and want to get into any
    discussions
we'll be forced to look into your position
vis-à-vis the Party.
You know the town's in trouble
and we expect you
yeah well.
We sat down and had a meal
with the Council Leader and my predecessor
and the next morning
I took over.
I had a lot of trouble at the beginning
with public speaking
that wasn't easy
and
other problems
getting housebuilding programmes finished
or food supplies
that was one of the biggest problems
we used to have in the DDR.
When the Mayor had to go off himself
to make sure there would be cheese in the shops
I don't even want to think about it
er
every fortnight
there would be these
Supply Commissions they were called
for the whole area.
And it was always about fruit and veg
and one of the things was sliced cheese.
Massive rows every time
I remember I'd made a big fuss
about how there was no cheese in Harzgerode.
And then the Chairman says:
But Manfred!
What the hell do you want!

I've got the list right in front of me!
Only last week you got 6 kilos of cheese for Harzgerode.
6 kilos!
6 kilos!
For a whole town!
That was what made those years
so terribly stressful.
The biggest disappointment for me
is that a well-ordered society
could collapse like that
as a result of so many subjective errors
and I have to keep saying this
that the principal errors happened within the Party.
That's what disappointed me most of all
because the social structure
was designed for the workers
and it was a good system
and the whole of this well-structured society
just collapsed.
And now!
Five years on!
What can I say about this town:
the town's finished!
Harzgerode has got 40% unemployment.
The people who were cursing us 5 years ago
denouncing us
have failed completely.
And now the situation is so difficult
and the demands on myself are so great
that yesterday I submitted nomination papers
and am going to stand
for Mayor of Harzgerode.
In Harzgerode we've had nothing
out of the wall comign down.
Except an Aldi
and that was a struggle.
The place is crippled.
There's nothing going on any more.
Hargerode used to be
the main town in the Quedlingburg area.
And now we have to be ashamed of ourselves.
If I'm elected:
I can use all the experience I've got
from being Mayor for 10 years of the DDR
I can use that again now.
In community politics.

Because in the DDR
we were good at community politics.
Here under this lime tree
is where I negotiated
the rebuilding of our school
with the chairman
of the planning authority.
It was January it was very cold
and we had an extra, private meeting
just the two of us
and I made him change his mind
the school had to be in Harzgerode after all.
My wife knows what I'm like.
She knows if I do it,
then it will go way beyond
what can be expected of honorary office
and she won't be seeing very much of me.
I'll be off early in the morning
and won't be back till late at night.
It's always been my greatest love
this town
and the people here
and that's a love I've never lost.

Factory Worker

I make the airbags
well just the parts
for the car airbags
the boss fetches them
and we clean them
cut off bits of waste
check them for holes
or blisters
and then they get soldered
it's a big business
I trained as a confectioner
nougat
we made nougat
for the West
nougat
it used to be exported to West Germany
our nougat
they used to sell it cheap over there
at Christmas time
and people would send it back to us
as Christmas presents
we always used to get
some of our nougat
from our Auntie in Rottweil
that's what used to happen
and we liked that
now I make airbags.

Professor

There's been such an extreme transformation
and so many changes
for me personally!
Well
I'll start at the beginning
For me it had always been a balancing act
between being afraid and toeing the line and a sort of measured
    er er criticism
especially when it came to political psychology
there were a couple of incidents
but they were much too tame
and other people were far braver
just among my closest friends
during that time I made a suggestion
that we set up a course in political psychology
I wrote a working paper
which was discussed here at the university
and as a result of this working paper
I was summoned to Berlin
in April 89
to the Central Committee building
it was the first time I'd been inside
it had these huge long corridors
and something happened there
which hurt me
very deeply
5 people sat in a row opposite me
shouting at me
trying to get me to change my mind
they wanted me to go to Leipzig
and teach a different subject
they wanted me out of social psychology here
and tried to tempt me by saying:
you can do political psychology there
as part of this related discipline
I knew
they wanted me away from this place
that was the main thing
I was still in the SED
and they had these Party commands
you couldn't refuse a command from the Party it wasn't done
I
when I did turn this down I said:
my wife is very ill

my wife
my wife at that time had er
a heart condition
she really wasn't well
I told them
that because I'd gone to Jena in 87
and she didn't want to come too
there'd already been a lot of trouble
because I'd been working very hard
it had caused a great deal of friction
I was very attached to my daughters
and I'd always spent a lot of time caring for them
though mainly at weekends
and if I now had to go to Leipzig
she definitely wouldn't go with me
and the marriage would break up
I didn't want that to happen
we had -
alright
maybe I was too jealous
I'd seen a lot which perhaps wasn't there
but I was simply afraid
of the marriage breaking up.
But they put me under such enormous pressure
also because of this working paper
that I
this is what really hurt me
that I cried in the presence of these 4 or 5 men
that they could cut me down so small
really hurt me.
They said: right,
you're going to have another think about this
because no-one disobeys a Party command!
And we'll discuss it once more
when your wife is well again
if not before.
Then came the Summer of 89
lots of people left the DDR
and a great deal happened
my best friend
Jakob in Berlin
was already in the opposition movement
and he told me: the time has come when we've got to do
    something.
I told him I was far too afraid
afraid for myself

afraid for my family
afraid for my job
but I'd started having real doubts
when so many people left the country.
Part of me was annoyed by them too.
I thought: why can't you stay here do something here!
Then in September I got ready
to go to Munich for a conference
on applied psychology.
The conference was at the beginning of October
from the 4th to the 10th of October 1989
in Munich
and we visited friends there too
a colleague a psychiatrist
we went to her house.
She said: let's eat later
first we've got to watch the news.
Afterwards she asked. 'How do you feel?
You can stay here if you want to.'
I told her: 'Now I really do have to go back!'
And...
yes we went back again
on the thirteenth
the Friday
I went to Berlin
I remember I went to my friend Jakob's house first
had a cup of coffee with him and a cigarette
I was shaking!
He said. 'Hey, what are you shaking for, man?
It's all over. It's finished. There's no need
to be afraid any more.'
I was still very nervous when I went along.
This time there were only two of them.
But it was very tough.
That conversation.
And very hurtful.
With all the old threats.
They still wanted me to go to Leipzig!
And all about my political psychology
and my visit to Munich.
I had to tell them everything that had happened in Munich.
Their manner was extremely unpleasant.
Right, they said, if you won't go to Leipzig
you'll not get a moment's peace in Jena.
That could have meant that
I would lose my job.

And because I'm anything but the resistant type
I have a nervous disposition
when they started using these sort of terms
I got very scared.
That was Friday the 13th!
By ten o'clock at night
I was back in Erfurt.
And my wife came out with:
'I'm sorry. That's it.'
And so the smaller family broke up too.
'It's no use,' she said.
'We can't go on.'
'You've been working so hard you never had any time.'
That's what she said. I didn't believe her.
Until I discovered that what I'd always thought was true.
Her present boyfriend
is the man who was her boss
he's 15 years older than her
more paternal
calmer
not as disorganized!
My whole world was falling apart.
I went mad
driving all over
the south of the DDR
in my Trabi
looking up friends
telling them what had happened to me.
I started smoking again
I've been doing it ever since
by mid-December I'd almost reached the point of saying:
What is there left?
What more do I want?
Everything was falling apart.
The family had collapsed.
How are you going to get yourself out of this hole?
Your ideas, your ideals, are all falling apart!
Despite all this
I have to say
as well as this manic-depressive cycle
there were also moments which were very different
driving here from Erfurt in the mornings
along the empty motorway:
Now you can think
things you've never been allowed to think before!
How many ideas were wrecked here by this institute!

Now you can do anything.
You can think and speak your mind.
And then the mood swung back again.
At the beginning of 1990
the restructuring proposals arrived
and of course I was worried
would I manage to make the jump?
Would I be accepted into the University?
How did I stand?
Well.
At least I've been able to carry on working.
I can say what I did
and I can also say when I was afraid.
I can breathe again.
I can go walking in the woods again.
No. I don't feel I've been punished.

Car Mechanic

I had this ladder outside
the doorway weren't finished
a big steep ladder
a wooden one
like a chicken ladder
and there were a knock at the kitchen here
I thought it were the ladder, it were always banging
but this lad were standing here
and he tells us
he's from one of these
no no
he dun't say nowt
he had a piece of paper
with it written down
that he cun't talk
that he's just learning to speak
he were trying to sell stuff
sponges
he had all sorts of identification
to show he were allowed to sell this stuff
from one of them factories they have for the handicapped
where they make things
and we bought a couple of sponges
13 Marks I paid him
you can get them in the shops for like 3.
10 of these glittery sponges there were
we thought we'd take one
we wun't send him away empty handed
so we got the sponges
and we still use them
come to think of it I think they cost more
we paid 14 Marks
well after that we said
if another one comes along
we'll chuck him down the stairs.
In Schwallungen recently
just recently
this bloke in a wheelchair
went round various people
one of them were the dentist
and he asks the dentist for a donation
because they've got money now those medical people
the dentist give him 20 or 30 Marks
and he made a right fuss

that it wun't enough
and he goes off in his wheelchair
next minute he stands up
walks over to a car
puts the wheelchair in the back
and drives off.
That were a month ago!
Fact!
Stood up, walked away and put his wheelchair in the boot!
All sorts of things go on!
In Wasungen
people come round
and we dun't have these things
little spyholes
in the front door
to look through
and one of these firms or some bloke
went round the flats
telling people
we're doing these spyholes
drilled holes in all their doors
took their money
and disappeared
he never come back.
Everyone got an hole in their door
and that were it.
Or these Italians
in cars
with leather jackets inside
there were
there were a big row here
we were outside in the yard
me and Fritz from next door
we were building a wall
working with cement
in summer
bare chests
and this car stops
a very respectable
middle-aged bloke
well dressed
in a jacket and tie
with all these leather jackets inside
and he asks us
we were standing there
bare chests

like I said
sweat pouring off us
and he tells us
he's just come from this trade fair
he's got to go back to Holland
and he dun't wanna take this stuff back with him
so he's gonna sell 'em off now dead cheap
leather jackets
they were so expensive here
and all that
so Fritz goes and says
er- I might be able to take one
and he tries one on
it were miles too big for him
but he's stood there
I can see him now trying to make it fit
hunching his shoulders
Oh that fits
if you put something on underneath
that'll fit fine
and then he goes and asks me
I told him if you wanna buy it that's your business.
How much is it then?
two hundred and fifty Marks
it's giving them away
so he goes in the house and gets two hundred and fifty Marks.
He never wears it
that jacket
must be at least three sizes too big.
When Cornelia come home
and he'd spent the last money they had
on that jacket
there were some row.
And that's the thing.
You never used to get conned like that before.
No-one was trying to rip you off
it just din't happen
and then suddenly it did.
Well.
The countryside's the same as before.

Engineer

The shift to the right is definitely there but I hope it's getting
stuck in its tracks. I haven't seen so much of it here because I
live further out in one of the new estates. But you do notice it
in certain places in Berlin. Certain people that you see. No,
no-one's had a go at me yet. But it happened to my husband.
Just after the wall came down. Somebody thought he looked
Jewish because he had one of those caps on. He's not a Jew,
he just happened to have one of these caps on. Wherever it
was somebody decided they were going to pick him out for
being Jewish and then they attacked him. Things like that
happen for no reason. He reported it.

He had a broken rib, various injuries, bruises and things, and it's
had other effects too. He's been a bit frightened ever since.
They shouted at him: you're a Jew! By the time words had
been said on both sides he was on the floor. And what's so
hard to understand about it is: there were people there, he
called for help and no-one did anything. It didn't used to be
like that. We had a community and it felt safer.

Chief Executive
(previously Politician in West Germany)

Well
I always say
let's not talk about the past
reunification is irreversible
you can be delighted you can be outraged
no-one's really bothered
so let's get on with putting the pieces back together!
These people need something to do.
They're happy when they have something.
And there's so much that needs to be done.
The key moment for me
was when I'd first come here
to Jena
and we had to make 16,000 people redundant
and I saw the old factories
where 5 people were carrying on pottering about
as if nothing had happened
and I told my people then
I've only just realised
we have to demolish these buildings
otherwise we'll have a disaster on our hands.
There'll be a handful of people in each room
fiddling away at something
and nothing will ever come of it.
We've got to act now
so that we can say:
the people have gone
the buildings have gone
now we need to rebuild
develop something new
something entirely different!
And when the people stood there
watching
us demolish the old factories in the city centre
and they said:
we survived the First World War and the Second World War
but we won't survive Späth
no
he's knocking everything down
I know
I almost cried too.
There was an old man by the gates
watching the big metal ball

smash through the walls on the fourth floor
and he said
I spent 30 years there
polishing lenses
the most beautiful lenses in the world
and he's knocking it all down!
So I went over and told him
I'm the one
who decided to knock that down
and he sort of apologized to me
and said
I wouldn't have said that so loud
if I'd known
you were standing right next to me.
I told him
that's quite alright you say what you like
to be honest
I feel very bad about doing this
but I know
that it's useless
if I start crying about the lenses too
because no-one buys them any more.
We have to build a shopping centre
or something like that
because now all the lenses get made in China.
Ah.
OK.
The man
was grateful
that I'd talked to him
we parted very amicably
but I'm sure he went away
shaking his head saying:
THIS HAS GOT TO BE THE END OF THE WORLD.

Frankfurt Christian Democrat and a dissatisfied worker

Christian Democrat What I like most about us in Germany is we've got certain principles of government and economic principles here which are worth maintaining, er what I mean is the er social market economy.

Worker If only we'd still got one! Kohl's completely destroyed it in the last ten years.

Christian Democrat Really.

Worker You've scrapped it, scrapped it in a thoroughly anti-social way.

Christian Democrat Who has? Who?

Worker You have. That Kohl government of yours.

Christian Democrat I'm not in the Kohl government. I voted for them!

Worker You voted for them. That makes you responsible for the whole mess.

Christian Democrat Who did you vote for? If you say I'm responsible. Who did you vote for!

Worker The man calls himself Adenauer's -

Christian Democrat Who was it! Who did you vote for! Who did you vote for!!

Worker Adenauer's -

Christian Democrat WHO DID YOU VOTE FOR!!

Worker Konrad Adenauer's grandson!

Christian Democrat WHO DID YOU VOTE FOR!!

Worker Do you know what Konrad Adenauer's greatest achievement was?

Christian Democrat Who did you vote for!!

Worker A state based on social justice. And you destroyed it.

Christian Democrat Who did you vote for! Stand by what you voted for.

Worker In the last parliamentary election?

Christian Democrat Yes?

Worker The party you'd probably find least er acceptable

Christian Democrat Just say it.

Worker No. Look. I voted for the SPD and the Greens. I split my vote because er well looking at it the other way there really isn't a party for workers to vote for in this state any more. To be perfectly frank all the parties

Christian Democrat You have no real understanding.

Worker I understand alright

Christian Democrat No, you don't understand.

Worker I understand right enough! I can see what you've done to our health system! I can see what you've done with our pensions! How you're financing the supposed reconstruction of the East! The poor people are the ones who have to pay! It's always the poor people!

Christian Democrat Everyone pays! Not just the poor!

Worker Solidarity levies mean we pay, the working man! It's obvious!

Christian Democrat No, it's not like that!

Worker Solidarity means the working man.

Christian Democrat Everyone pays!

Worker No they don't! The workers are the ones who are paying.

Christian Democrat Everyone does!

Worker We do, the working people. Whether it's unemployment benefit! Or pension or health insurance! The largest single expense a working man has in a city like Frankfurt is rent! And you have the most anti-social housing policy any federal government has ever had. How many homes are you going to build!

Christian Democrat You don't have to shout. The words mean exactly the same. The louder you shout the less I can hear you.

Worker You're cutting back on nursery places. You have to be dying now to qualify for a prescription!

Christian Democrat We all have to make sacrifices. Every one of us!

Worker That would be a fine thing. If you really did mean everyone. For me that means someone who earns a lot pays more than someone who doesn't. And that isn't a special solidarity levy! Then it gets paid for out of taxes...

Christian Democrat Alright, but I'm sure you're not really paying all that much! Not so much that it justifies this huge palaver! I'm sure every month you spend two or three times as much money on things that at the end of the month you know you spent it but you've no idea where the money went. And you're in exactly the same position as a lot of other people I know: they've got money for Coca-Cola, they eat at McDonalds, for all I know they go to prostitutes and the reason they never have any money is because they spend it on the wrong things.

Worker Prostitutes? Well, I can assure you. That is not true in my case.

Christian Democrat The reason you don't have any money is because you spend it on the wrong things.

Worker No!

Christian Democrat No!! You don't have any money because you spend it on the wrong things!!

Local Reporter
(previously Member of DDR Politburo)

It's all been gone over so often now
all been said
supposedly. This stuff about I got a memo
that evening: 'Günter. Open the border.'
and so forth, load of rubbish
er
because the memo
there didn't need to be a memo
because
we had the say
in those days
we took the decision
I was one of the three
who deposed Honecker
that's right
we had the say
Well. That's all in the past.
This is where I am now.
As I was saying
I've had the good fortune
to get out of that armour-plated ideology
to escape
those ties are very strong
and this is where I've landed
it's a local paper, run purely on advertising
in Nordhessen
near the old border
on the western side
I have to earn money I have to support my family
who as I was saying are still in Berlin
and this was a chance
otherwise
I didn't have a chance
the paper can only exist
as a free sheet
so we stick to what's going on locally
being a local paper means
we have to stick to local matters.
Right
what is it about Germany
I like most
well
to be quite honest I've got to say

that's a question
that I don't really have much sympathy for
yes well
well
that was never important to me
when I talk about Germany
I can only think of this Germany
the single Germany
that exists now
for me basically
it's never been so much a question of Germany
and the Germans
for me
and the influence is obvious
the main question
has always been the system
Germany my God Germany
that's always been a dodgy idea
when you look at the workers' movement
then
the workers
er
they were always an international movement
that was their great strength
nationalism was Bismarck
nationalism was spiked helmets
the police
the nationalists were bourgeois
little domestic tyrants.
The workers didn't live in beautiful countryside
they were in dark holes
staying in rented rooms
they were never able to cultivate
this feeling of *Heimat*,
this sentimental attachment to the countryside.
It wasn't Germany that I was looking for
when I came here to this little paper
I wanted to understand this other, more durable system
though
for the first time in my life
I drove
in every possible direction
to Bavaria to Hamburg
all over the place
and then
a grandeur

which I had never really been aware of before
which was this idea of *Heimat*
suddenly began to mean something to me
I actually caught myself feeling it
driving through these places
I began to understand why
people do feel an affinity for these landscapes
well to a certain extent I've
driven it out of myself
driven through that
and out the other side
though of course I've always had a soft spot
for Brandenburg
but that was quite
er
er
practical
so
it wasn't so much a beautiful landscape that I saw as:
'It's nice to have a lake here so people can go swimming.'
That's typical of this kind of utilitarian thinking
which divides the world into
useful
non-useful
essential
non-essential
and here I came up against a different way of thinking:
that existence is its own justification
that's something I only really understood here
all that messing around with projections
the plan says this
this must be achieved
by a particular time
and all the stress that followed
because it never was achieved on time
and we used to have to change the plan again afterwards
to make it fit.
That was a real eye-opener for me.
So then I started reading
and this has been one of the most shaming discoveries I've ever
    made
that everything I'm starting to piece together now
things I'm gradually coming to recognize as weaknesses
the causes of our failure
had been known 30 years ago
and all the details written down

I'm the kind of person
who can be profoundly affected by literature
so Koestler
Darkness at Noon
had the hairs standing up on the back of my neck
reading that did.
It shows the way that kind of ideology
destroys people's minds.
That's the drama
the crime
if you want to call it that -
but it's also
a human drama!
We never set out
to be criminals.
Even a man like Honecker isn't a criminal
he was a limited person
a fanatical worker
a proletarian
who tried to change something
though
with a narrowness
which was characteristic of his type.
As critical of him
as I am
I find it very difficult to see what he did
as a crime.
I think it's a dreadful error, a horrendous mistake,
though that offers little comfort to those who were affected.

Old Lady from Weimar

Oh this is the most beautiful country
and I like everything about it
it's all wonderful
I always look on the bright side
and I've been thrilled by the way we've been making up for all
    that time
that was er
I have to say er
it was er
er well!
The top people! They've all been here!
The things we did in the years
when everything was in ruins
I am from Weimar
but I came here originally from Frankfurt
yes I'm very pleased, very pleased
yes
yes
only the escalators go a bit fast
they're too fast for an old woman.
What I like most are the writers.
The best ones are all dead.
My favourite is
er er
Faust!
Our highest achievement.
Faust!
The Prologue in Heaven.

Die Sonne tönt nach alter Weise
In Brudersphären Wettgesang,
Und ihre vorgeschriebne Reise
Vollendet sie mit Donnerklang.
Ihr Anblick gibt den Engeln Stärke,
Wenn keiner sie ergründen mag;
Die unbegreiflich hohen Werke
Sind herrlich wie am ersten Tag.

Do you know *Faust*?

Security Guard

Germany?
What I love
about Germany?
Love?
That's a difficult question.
Too difficult
it might be misinterpreted
if I say beer
er
that what I like most about Germany is the beer
that's er
my er
favourite
you see if I say beer
then someone might get the idea
all the Germans are alcoholics
and that's why er
I'd have to think about it
but just like off the cuff
here
no
I've got work to do!

Master Painter

Over the other side of the Neisse
that's where I was born
in Prager Strasse
I don't get any dole money
or a pension
because I missed so many years
now
I'm stuck here with no money
I'm behind with the electricity
and the rent.
By the end of the month
it could be that I'm out on the streets
dunno where I'd go
I got rehabilitated two and a half months ago
I spent 5 years inside in the DDR
just cos I wanted to go
from Germany to Germany.
I was born here in Görlitz
in 33
did an apprenticeship as a painter
and when I'd done me training
the boss said: 'Sorry, but I can't
pay you fully qualified.'
It was just after the war
that lasted about 5 months
then I was conscripted to go to Wismut
uranium mine
aye
that's where I worked
the conditions were very primitive
they had none of them underground train things
if a load tipped over
you had to get your back behind it
and right it again yourself
it was terrible
I wanted to get out of there
aye
I did too
got over the border
to the West
near Hof
that was the beginning of 1950
and I got down as far as Nürnberg.
According to Eastern law I was of age at 18

but according to Western law I wouldn't till I was 21
so the first thing they did over there in West Germany
was lock us up
for not having valid papers
and crossing the border illegally.
That meant the West officially recognized
the border with the Eastern zone.
Yeah and they stuck us in a youth home
then one day
they shoved us back over the border
in Sonneberg
in the *Stasi* prison
one interrogation after another
'Why did you come back over?'
'They sent you.'
'You're a Western spy!'
'You're an agent for American intelligence!'
aye
that was how the whole thing started
I tried to escape again
through Czechoslovakia this time
and the Czechs caught us at the border
and they took me down to Joachimstal
and put us in the Czech *Stasi* prison
which was a bit more decent than the German ones
aye
I had to spend 6 weeks working in a porcelain factory
once I'd done my six weeks
I was tried
sentenced again
this time to 6 months
for crossing the border illegally
aye
when those six months were up
I was put on a transport
over the border back to Aue
and into the hands of the State Security Service.
And they
the first thing they did
was give us a right doing over
It was the first time I'd ever been seriously beaten up
they used their hands
they used their fists
ha ha
they treated us like scum
kicked me here there

So then I tried to escape again
like a cat I climbed
right up the inside the light well
in no time I'm on the roof
and over the wall
and by coincidence I met someone
I'd used to work with
I said: you've got to help us out.
Yeah, what is it?
I said the *Stasi* had been keeping us locked up
I'd got out
and I needed some cash
alright, he says,
I'll help you
I'll meet you back here in two hours' time
and he went straight to the police
escaped prisoner
and all this
I went back to meet him two hours later
police
back inside
kept us in the dark this time
5 months in the cells
with the *Stasi*
worn down day and night
in the end I
signed everything
they put in front of me
just so they would leave us alone
then I had time to start wondering
what have I gone and signed now?
Did I just sign my own death sentence?
So I went on hunger strike.
Aye
on the second day
the officer came down
who'd interrogated us
the prisoners called him 'Rat-ear'
he was a nasty piece of work, a right bastard
Stasi Major he was
a bullet had grazed the side of his head
and left him with just the one ear.
He came down to my cell
'Why aren't you eating?'
the guard was there
with a big aluminium bowl.

When I told him: I'm not eating
he still brought the bowl in
boiling hot it was
I picked the bowl up
and threw it straight in his face
it went all over his uniform.
He screamed
'You wait, you pig.
I'll get you for that.
You won't forget this in a hurry.'
He was shouting, wiping the soup off his face.
About an hour later
two guards came down and got us
blindfolded us
and made us crawl up the stairs on all fours
I said I want to withdraw my statement!
You can't withdraw anything
the sentence has already been passed.
'Strip.'
It was the middle of winter
the cell was roughly so high
and there was a wall
I had to climb over the wall
and I wondered what's going to happen now.
Door shut.
And I could hear running water
they'd turned the water on from outside
it started getting higher and higher
and when the water got as high as the wall
I was standing there up to my chest in this icy liquid.
I kept tight hold of that wall
and kept swapping my weight from one leg to the other
so I didn't collapse
with exhaustion
I was really scared
I thought I would drown
in this horrible stuff.
In the morning
around eight
the water suddenly went away
they let it drain off
took us outside
gave us a hot shower
clothes on
then I was taken to Chemnitz
to a normal prison

yeah it was February 51
when I was sentenced.
Prosecutor Bauch
he was big in the Party
gold Party badge
complete bastard
the stuff
he came out with
in his summing up he said:
'Nothing can be proved against the accused
he has only been suspected of these crimes
I would recommend 6 years' imprisonment
and 5 years' punishment in the community!'
My collar practically burst
I jumped to my feet
and said
Prosecutor! can you open the window
and let a little justice in here.
Nothing proved and 6 years in prison in the same breath?
They could twist everything round any way they wanted
it wasn't a public hearing
it was a schoolroom
rows of benches
and a long table at the front
with a smaller table in front of it
where I sat
it was obvious
there was no practical solution
I'd been marked down
the verdict had been fixed before it all began
and then there was someone from the trade union
addressed us
'You're one of a large family. All workers. How could you do
    this to our state! Our workers' and peasants' state! To your
    own family!'
I said what's that got to do with it?
I wanted to go from Germany to Germany!
'You can't say that. We are a separate, independent state.' Blah
    blah blah.
Aye
I was put on a transport to Waldheim.
To start with I was in solitary
then after a few weeks I was put in a cell with 3 others
4 men in a cell for one
shit bucket in the corner
aye

from 51 to January 56 I was in Waldheim
and then I was put on another transport
to Hohenschönhausen
in East Berlin
it was a work camp for the Ministry of State Security
the food was very good
we were allowed to grow our hair again there
and we were given cigarettes
aye
then one day
on the building site
in 56
it was midday
we'd just sat down to eat
and a lorry came to fetch us
numbered roll call
14 were released that day
and I was the last one on the list
the night before I'd had a dream
I'd seen exactly what would happen
an officer comes with a list
calls out the names
and one of them's mine.
Hans they're letting you out today!
Rubbish, I said!
I've got another 14 months to do yet!
But it was true.
Went in
had a medical
showered
then we got civvies
they didn't have a jacket that would fit
so I got a ladies' jacket that had been altered
a blue one
with blue Army trousers
and a woollen scarf
an old Russian greatcoat
and one of those poodle caps
with those big flaps over the ears.
When you come out
in Rummelsburg
there's a big open square
at the other end of this open square
is the underground station
there was a train just pulling in
I jumped on

I'd had a quick look to check
it was going to West Berlin
and I sat there
really nervous
there was an old man sitting opposite
he said:
You're from the East aren't you?
From prison?
Have you escaped?
I told him, yes.
He said: get off at the next station
you're in West Berlin
and I managed to get off
without anyone noticing.
I came to a baker's
and I could see the windows were full
of cakes and gateau
and I couldn't stop myself
I just stood there in front of it all and cried.
Eventually I went in with my fifty EastMarks
and said I'd like a couple of slices of cake please
she sees my money and says:
'I'm sorry
we don't take Eastern money here.
But what sort of state are you in?
Where've you come from?'
I've just got out of prison
'You poor thing, come in here'
and she took us into the kitchen
and she gave us a cup of coffee
and a big plate of cake
and told me: 'Eat it, silly, as much as you want,
as much as you can get down you.'
She made sure I was properly fed.
I went to the circus next
Circus Busch
in the West
I went in there
and asked if they had any work.
Yes, if you've got Western papers.
Have you got a trade?
I say I'm a painter and I can do other stuff too.
He said: sorry
not if you haven't got Western papers.
Otherwise I'd take you on right now.
Aye

on the other side of the street there's a police station
passport police
and of course their jaws just dropped
I said: what should I do now
they took us by bus to the airport
and flew us straight out
er
to er
West Germany
and we landed in Hannover
from Hannover they took us to Ülzen
to a camp
there was a medical examination
I was 70% unfit for work
I had a severe heart disorder
stomach ulcers
light tuberculosis
and problems with my circulation.
I got my first Western identity card there
800 Marks to keep us going
and I went to Hamburg.
I'd met a girl in the refugee camp
she was from Hamburg originally
and we got married on 31st December 1956
everyone told us
it's a New Year prank
it'll never work
and one day I had a seizure
she'd told us she was in a special condition
she was pregnant
and I'd been so happy
until it turns out
it wasn't my child
and then she had an abortion
I screamed like a madman
after that I met another woman
and soon after the divorce I married her
and at that time there was a real campaign in Hamburg
you refugees from the East get everything
and we good people of Hamburg get nothing.
The Hamburg people were so envious
it made us ill.
So my wife and I emigrated
let's do something else I said
with a bit of work we'll be ok
aye

I went to Australia
on the MS Aurelia
sick as a dog all the way.
I spent 30 years in Australia
working as a painter
aye
then we saw the wall on television
the uprisings there were here
in Hungary, Poland, all over
we saw them on television.
Right, I told myself,
now it's time to go back to Germany.
I've not seen my mother in more than 40 years
so now I'll go over and see what's up
there's bound to be work
bound to be some way of earning money
so on 19th February 1990
I came back to Görlitz
and my mother
she's already 85.
I said: there's got to be something to do here.
So I went self-employed
I had adverts running in all the local papers for 6 months
and I got work
it came from all sides
at first on my own
then I had one man
then three
five
and in May last year I was employing 12 people.
Then suddenly the bank foreclosed on us
credit stopped
accounts frozen
because I was owed so much I couldn't continue
and I'd only been paying net wages
there was tax and insurance
and some materials hadn't been paid for.
Now I'm still owed 40,000 Marks
and I can't get it back.
My firm's bust.
And here I am.

Actor

Er
it's
it's
it's
personal
er because
I stopped drinking that day
on 9th November
on 9th November exactly
yeah
yeah
no no
I didn't
I didn't know
I hadn't heard
I was in hospital
it was a coincidence
dunno
fate
I don't believe in fate
but
it was such a coincidence
that the day I had to
er
stop
the wall came down
I woke up
and I was
doubly
doubly a new person
I started to live without drinking
and in a new society
I'd been drinking
let me think
around ten glasses of beer
and half a bottle of brandy
up to a bottle a day
and it ruined my circulation
I was taken to hospital
and
I dunno
it was like
like
my mum came

and my dad
I was in bed
and
I could see
they'd brought oranges
and I told them:
you shouldn't have
they're pensioners
they could go over
but
I said
it's not Christmas
where did you get the oranges?
You shouldn't have gone to the West
it's not -
No, they said, no
it's not Christmas
but the border's open
yes.
Well
I wondered where I was
whether I was in heaven
but no
I had all my wits about me.
Still
it felt pretty strange.

An Instant Playscript

Waiting Room Germany first published
in Great Britain in 1995 as a paperback original
by Nick Hern Books Ltd, 14 Larden Road, London W3 7ST
in association with the Royal Court Theatre, London,
and by arrangement with Rowohlt Verlag, Hamburg

Wartesaal Deutschland Stimmenreich
copyright © 1995 Rotbuch Verlag, Hamburg

Translation from the German copyright © 1995 David Tushingham

Klaus Pohl and David Tushingham have asserted their right to be
identified respectively as the author and the translator of this work

Text typeset by the translator
Re-formatted to publisher's specification
by Country Setting, Woodchurch, Kent TN26 3TB

Printed and bound in Great Britain

ISBN 1 85459 274 2

A CIP catalogue record for this book is available from
the British Library

*The text published here was generated directly from the translator's
own typescript on 1 November 1995, when the play was in rehearsal.
It may therefore differ slightly from the text as performed.*